T0098368

Improving Perkins II Performance Measures and Standards

Lessons Learned from Early Implementers in Four States

Brian M. Stecher, Lawrence M. Hanser,
and Bryan Hallmark, RAND

Mikala L. Rahn, Karen Levesque, E. Gareth Hoachlander,
David Emanuel, and Steven G. Klein,
MPR Associates, Inc.

RAND, Santa Monica, CA

National Center for Research in Vocational Education
University of California, Berkeley
1995 University Avenue, Suite 375
Berkely, CA 94704-1306

Supported by
The Office of Vocational and Adult Education,
U.S. Department of Education

FUNDING INFORMATION

Project Title: National Center for Research in Vocational Education

Grant Number: V051A30004-93A/V051A30003-93A

Act Under Which
Funds Administered: Carl D. Perkins Vocational Education Act
P.L. 98-524

Source of Grant: Office of Vocational and Adult Education
U.S. Department of Education
Washington, D.C. 20202

Grantee: The Regents of the University of California
c/o National Center for Research in Vocational
Education
2150 Shattuck Ave., Suite 1250
Berkeley, CA 94704

Director: Charles S. Benson

Percent of Total Grant
Financed by Federal Money: 100%

Dollar Amount of
Federal Funds for Grant: $6,000,000

Disclaimer: This publication was prepared pursuant to a grant with the Office of Vocational and Adult Education, U.S. Department of Education. Grantees undertaking such projects under government sponsorship are encouraged to express freely their judgment in professional and technical matters. Points of view or opinions do not, therefore, necessarily represent official U.S. Department of Education position or policy.

Discrimination: Title VI of the Civil Rights Act of 1964 states: "No person in the United States shall, on the ground of race, color, or national origin, be excluded from participation in, be denied the benefits of, or be subjected to discrimination under any program or activity receiving federal financial assistance." Title IX of the Education Amendments of 1972 states: "No person in the United States shall, on the basis of sex, be excluded from participation in, be denied the benefits of, or be subjected to discrimination under any education program or activity receiving federal financial assistance." Therefore, the National Center for Research in Vocational Education project, like every program or activity receiving financial assistance from the U.S. Department of Education, must be operated in compliance with these laws.

The Carl D. Perkins Vocational and Applied Technology Education Act of 1990 (Perkins II) contained a number of significant changes from previous federal vocational education legislation. The act required states to develop outcome-based accountability systems built around statewide performance measures and standards. States were given considerable flexibility in identifying outcomes to be measured, selecting measurement tools, and setting standards. Local programs were given the principal responsibility for program improvement, with states intervening only when local programs were unable to demonstrate significant progress. Measures and standards were supposed to be adopted by the fall of 1992 and used thereafter as accountability tools and guides to program improvement.

This study is one of a series of investigations conducted by the National Center for Research in Vocational Education (NCRVE) relating to vocational education accountability and the implementation of these measures and standards. The present research focuses on the effects of the performance measures and standards on state vocational education agencies, local programs, and the relationships between them. The study examines four states that were among the first to adopt measures and standards and implement data collection and reporting systems. Information gathered from these states gives some indication of the impact of the legislation among "early adopters" and the factors that affect implementation. The findings should be of interest to federal policymakers considering the reauthorization of the legislation, as well as to state and local vocational educators looking for ways to improve the utility of their accountability systems.

CONTENTS

TABLES

States have had three years to implement the accountability and program improvement provisions of the Carl D. Perkins Vocational and Applied Technology Education Act of 1990 (Perkins II). This study examined progress in implementing statewide systems of performance measures and standards, the effects of these systems on state agencies and local vocational programs, and the factors that influenced state and local actions.[1] We offer recommendations for changes in federal policy to promote the goals of local accountability and program improvement embodied in the original legislation.

PROCEDURES

We selected four states that were "early adopters" of measures and standards for study. In each state, we interviewed staff in the state agency (or agencies) that administered secondary and postsecondary vocational education and visited secondary and postsecondary vocational institutions in two geographically separated regions. Each institution was visited twice, once in the fall of 1993 and again in the spring of 1994. During the site visits, we interviewed administrators and instructors in each institution.

---

[1]No formal attempt was made to determine whether states were in compliance with Perkins II or to judge the quality of the measures and standards states had chosen to implement.

WHAT WE FOUND

Substantial progress has been made in implementing measures and standards in the states that were visited, although much work remains to be done to make the systems function as envisioned in the law. By 1994, little attention had been paid to building state- or local-level capacity for translating the measures and standards data into actions at the local level for program improvement. These "leading edge" states were still largely engaged in developing and implementing their systems.

Furthermore, wide variation was found in the states' approaches to the development and implementation of measures and standards. This variation was evident in almost every aspect of program implementation, including how the process was managed, who participated, and the level of resources devoted to it. These differences appeared to be jointly a function of the states' individuality and the flexibility inherent in Perkins II.

WHAT EXPLAINS PROGRESS TO DATE?

We identified several factors that contributed to the variation in state responses to performance measures and standards. Some of these explanatory factors are within the sphere of influence of federal policy, including:

- **Flexibility provided to the states in the law itself.** The flexibility of the Perkins II mandate for measures and standards had mixed effects. It permitted states to create systems that were responsive to local conditions, but it also increased the influence of state and local contextual factors on implementation, which slowed and limited the process in some cases.

- **Unclear integration and coordination of Perkins II provisions.** In the states we visited, the Perkins II priorities—measures and standards, integration, tech-prep education,[2] and service to

---

[2]"The term 'tech-prep education program' means a combined secondary and post-secondary program which leads to an associate degree or 2-year certificate; provides technical preparation in at least 1 field of engineering technology, applied science, mechanical, industrial, or practical art or trade, or agriculture, health, or business;

special populations—were treated as separate activities. They were not seen as a coordinated system at either the state or local level, and performance measures and standards were not being used comprehensively to evaluate the other Perkins initiatives.

- **Lack of models or incentives for state and local implementation.** Perkins II contains an explicit framework for structuring systems and federal agency checks for compliance at the adoption stage, but there are neither models nor incentives for ensuring that performance measures and standards are used to improve programs.

- **Limited expertise and resources at the state level.** Perkins II created new responsibilities for state staff while reducing the set-aside for state administration. This presented a dilemma for some states that lacked both the expertise and the resources to address these new demands.

- **Mandated measurement of learning outcomes.** The scarcity of valid assessment tools for measuring selected learning outcomes led states to adopt alternatives that were less than optimal. States are still struggling with how to measure important student outcomes, such as academic skill gains at the postsecondary level.

The second set of factors flows from state and local context, and hence, these factors are less directly subject to federal policy intervention. These included the choice betweem a centralized and a local implementation strategy, the existence of statewide data systems, the availability of state-level assessment tools, the nature of ongoing educational accountability and program review mechanisms, historical relationships among state and local educational and employment agencies, attempts to reduce the burden on local administrators, and the influence of key administrators.

---

builds student competence in mathematics, science, and communications (including through applied academics) through a sequential course of study; and leads to placement in employment." (The Carl D. Perkins Vocational and Applied Technology Education Act Amendments of 1990. P.L. 101–392; Part E, Sec. 347.)

Finally, there are issues on the horizon that will affect the implementation of measures and standards and should be considered in planning the reauthorization of Perkins:

- **Skill standards and curriculum standards.** The Departments of Education and Labor are funding the development of industry skill standards in more than 20 occupational areas and curriculum standards in six educational fields. There should be some coordination between these efforts and the systems of measures and standards developed under Perkins II.

- **Data quality.** States have not yet addressed the questions of reliability and validity of the measurement tools they have selected. Data quality questions will become more important as states begin the accountability and program improvement cycle, which will add high stakes to the performance measures and standards.

- **Integration of academic and vocational education.** The integration of academic and vocational education raises a host of problems for defining, measuring, and attributing outcomes and therefore threatens the validity of existing systems of measures and standards.

- **Consistency in federal vocational education policy.** Some state vocational educators believe new laws will supplant many of the initiatives contained in Perkins II; as a result, they make only halfhearted efforts at implementation. In this way, the volatility of federal vocational education policy discourages rapid and effective response to federal initiatives.

RECOMMENDATIONS

Federal policymakers may take several actions to enhance the future success of performance-based accountability in vocational education and promote the goals of Perkins II:

- **Clarify the interrelationships among Perkins II mandates and the coordination of Perkins II initiatives.** Perkins II contains four major priorities: integrating vocational and academic education, providing service to special populations, creating tech-prep education programs, and establishing systems of measures and standards. Two of these are primarily curricular changes;

one relates to the selection of students; and one relates to accountability and program improvement. In theory, these efforts should complement one another, and states' efforts to address the priorities should be coordinated. In fact, none of the four states coordinated their efforts to address these mandates, and there was wide variation in the relative priority assigned to these four critical initiatives. Policymakers should clarify the interrelationships among systems of measures and standards, the integration of academic and vocational education, tech-prep education programs, and service to special populations and offer additional guidance about coordinating states' efforts in these areas.

- **Create models for outcome-based program improvement.** In 1994, most state action was still driven by the mandate to develop a structure for accountability, i.e., the system of measures and standards. Little had been done to use that structure to make programs better. State and local agencies need assistance in translating outcome deficiencies into action plans. One approach might be to require states to develop program improvement models that illustrate how outcome-based information can be used for local program reform. The alternative we suggest would be to commission an agency other than the states themselves to collect examples of effective outcome-based local improvement practices and disseminate them widely for states and local programs to use.

- **Provide focused technical assistance regarding choices and resources.** The "flexible mandates" of Perkins II place greater demands on state agencies yet restrict the use of funds for state-level services. These fiscal restrictions come at a time when many state administrative budgets are also being reduced. Under these circumstances, federal actions that help states respond to their choices and make better use of resources might significantly improve implementation of the act. We also suggest increasing the funds available for state administration during the start-up phase, so states can meet initial demands and develop some of the expertise they will need to operate a reformed vocational education system.

- **Address common measurement problems.** The technology to measure learning and occupational performance gains in reliable, valid, and efficient ways is not widely available. Most states are not equipped with either the resources or expertise to develop tools for measuring learning and occupational outcomes, and it is unfair to require them to accomplish this difficult task. The federal government needs to assume leadership in addressing these problems, since they are best solved nationally and are largely the result of the provisions of Perkins II.

Incorporating these changes into the reauthorization of federal vocational education legislation will increase the efficacy of statewide systems of measures and standards. Legislators also should anticipate difficulties and conflicts that may be created by pending reforms of education, training, and workforce preparedness programs and should work to coordinate the accountability requirements of all these initiatives.

ACKNOWLEDGMENTS

This study is based on interviews with state and local vocational educators in four states. Our promise of anonymity prevents us from naming the states and the individuals but not from recognizing the central role they played in this research. We want to thank the four state directors of vocational education and the staff in the four state vocational education agencies. We also want to acknowledge the assistance of the administrators, instructors, and other staff in the secondary schools and community colleges we visited.

Chapter One

INTRODUCTION

It has been three years since states began to implement the account-ability and program improvement provisions of the Carl D. Perkins Vocational and Applied Technology Education Act of 1990 (Perkins II), and policymakers are asking whether these provisions are work-ing. We know, from previous National Center for Research in Vocational Education (NCRVE) research, that states adopted systems of measures and standards as prescribed by federal law (Rahn et al., 1992), but we do not know whether, or how well, these systems were implemented, or whether they are leading to program improvement. These two questions are particularly relevant at present, because it is time for the reauthorization of federal vocational education legisla-tion. Policymakers are looking for information about the success of these locally focused, outcome-based systems of program improve-ment and about ways to improve the federal rules that govern them.

This study examines the implementation of Perkins II performance measures and standards to date and, based on this interim review, recommends actions the federal government can take to improve these systems. Ultimately, Perkins II should be judged in terms of outcomes: Has the legislation established and/or strengthened local systems of outcome-based program review and improvement, and have these systems led to improved workforce outcomes at the local level?

However, it may be too soon to make these judgments. States are only now entering the first program improvement cycle, and widespread data on outcomes are at least one to two years away.

Consequently, we framed our research in terms of two more immediate questions:

- Are states implementing their systems of measures and standards as envisioned in the federal legislation?

- What factors have affected their progress, and can progress be enhanced through federal action?

Before presenting our results, we provide some background on the requirements of Perkins II and on relevant NCRVE research.

LEGISLATIVE REQUIREMENTS

Perkins II called for the creation of performance-based state accountability systems for improving vocational programs. One of the most dramatic changes in Perkins II was the addition of outcome-based performance measures and standards in these accountability systems, particularly the inclusion of learning outcomes that were seldom specified in previous evaluations of vocational programs.

Perkins II required each state to "develop and implement a statewide system of core standards and measures of performance" by September 1992 (Public Law 101-392, Section 115(a)). The mandate has three key distinguishing features: (1) It emphasizes the use of outcomes to monitor program success; (2) it gives states considerable flexibility in creating systems; and (3) it assigns primary responsibility for program improvement to local programs.

At minimum, each state was required to include in its system at least two sets of measures. The first must be a measure of "learning and competency gains, including student progress in achieving basic and more advanced academic skills." The other set must include any one of the following four measures: (1) competency attainment; (2) job or work skill attainment; (3) retention or completion in school; or (4) placement in further education, the military, or employment.

Although Perkins II prescribes the basic guidelines that states must follow in designing accountability systems, it also provides each state considerable discretion in developing and implementing a system that fits its individual situation and needs. For example, some states have taken a centralized approach to designing their measures, prescribing specific assessment instruments or data collection procedures to be used by local recipients, while others have taken a decentralized approach, charging local recipients to develop their own instruments or procedures. At the time of our research, states had not all reached the same stage of implementation of their selected systems of measures and standards.

PRIOR NCRVE RESEARCH

Since Perkins II was enacted, NCRVE has been actively involved in providing technical assistance to state-level administrators to assist them in developing and implementing systems of performance measures and standards. NCRVE researchers wrote a guidebook, *Accountability for Vocational Education: A Practitioner's Guide* (Hoachlander, Levesque, and Rahn, 1992), which was distributed at regional workshops and has been widely used by state-level administrators to explore key issues in designing an accountability system.

NCRVE researchers also examined several local vocational education accountability systems to gather information that might help improve the implementation of Perkins II. *Beyond Vocational Education Standards and Measures: Strengthening Local Accountability Systems for Program Improvement* (Stecher and Hanser, 1993) described local accountability systems that already existed for many vocational programs and showed how those systems could be used for program improvement. The authors suggested ways that states and local programs might improve the functioning of local accountability systems.

Continuing interest in obtaining information about state responses to the performance measures and standards requirements led NCRVE to compile *State Systems for Accountability in Vocational Education* (Rahn, Hoachlander, and Levesque, 1992). This report contains a summary of the performance measures and standards implemented by states in the fall of 1992 and provides examples of clearly defined measures and standards. The appendix briefly describes each state's system of performance measures and standards at both the secondary and postsecondary levels. The report is based not only on information gathered through workshops and telephone interviews but also on analysis of documentation submitted to NCRVE.

OVERVIEW

This study examines how some states are progressing in achieving the accountability goals outlined in Perkins II. It focuses on the process of implementing performance measures and standards for vocational education at the state and local levels. It is too soon to tell how the implementation will work out in these states, let alone to know whether the systems will have the desired effects of institutionalizing local outcome-based program improvement systems. Nevertheless, results to date can be used to judge the degree to which states are succeeding in achieving the vision embodied in Perkins II, what factors affected their progress, and how federal legislation might promote greater success in the future.

In this study, no attempt was made to judge whether the states were in *compliance* with the legislation. The Office of Vocational and Adult Education (OVAE) is the agency responsible for determining compliance, not NCRVE. Moreover, no formal assessment was made of the *quality* of the measures and standards themselves in these states. Perkins II requires the Secretary of Education to submit a report to Congress that assesses "the validity, predictiveness, and reliability" of standards and measures. The secretary's report may include some measures of quality.

Our report is organized as follows. Chapter Two briefly describes the research procedures. Chapter Three presents findings regarding state implementation and includes brief summaries of the evolution of performance measures and standards at the secondary and postsecondary levels in each state. Chapter Four discusses the factors that affected states' actions, including both conditions that may be subject to federal actions and local and state contextual factors that are within the domain of state policy. The discussion also identifies emerging conditions that are likely to affect the implementation of Perkins II in the near future. The final chapter recommends actions to enhance the implementation of these systems.

Chapter Two

PROCEDURES

SAMPLING

A small purposive sample of four states was chosen to develop a deeper understanding of the implementation of Perkins II measures and standards from states that were farthest along in the process as of January 1993 (Rahn, Hoachlander, and Levesque, 1992). This sampling strategy has two advantages. First, it permits us to extrapolate and draw inferences from states that have completed more of the required steps in establishing outcome-based accountability systems. That is, because these states are further along, they have greater experience with more aspects of the system and its implementation. Second, and as a direct result of their experiences, our strategy enables us to identify models that might inform other states and improve their systems. For example, state and local strategies that worked in our sample of states might be adopted by states struggling with implementation.

The major disadvantage of this strategy is that the four states are not necessarily representative of the country as a whole. Conditions in these four states might not be duplicated in others, and actions that worked here might be less successful elsewhere. As a result, the reader should be cautious about extrapolating these findings or interpreting them as representative of the country as a whole. While the findings from the four states in our sample may not be generalizable, we believe our recommendations, if implemented, would benefit many states in their implementations of Perkins II.

DATA COLLECTION

In each state, we visited the state department of education and selected secondary and postsecondary institutions in two different regions. The secondary and postsecondary institutions we visited in these regions were chosen by the state, in consultation with us. We asked the state departments of education to choose institutions typical for their state. We also asked for variety in terms of economic conditions and encouraged the states to choose one urban and one rural region.

A team of two researchers spent a total of approximately one and one-half weeks in each state over the course of two visits (Fall 1993, Spring 1994). At the school districts, we spoke with administrators and instructors and asked about the implementation of Perkins II and its effects. We developed a structured interview guide with tailored questions for chief administrators (including district superintendents, college chancellors, and college presidents), principals, directors of vocational education (including college vocational administrators), and instructors. After determining his or her familiarity with the state-adopted system of measures and standards, we questioned each interviewee on the following topics:

- The importance of measures and standards vis-à-vis other vocational education initiatives (For example, which vocational education reforms or initiatives received the most emphasis in your institution in the past two years?)

- The integration of vocational education accountability with other educational reforms (For example, is accountability an important aspect of general education reform? If so, how have vocational education measures and standards affected this process or been affected by it?)

- Implementation of measures and standards (For example, what steps have been taken to implement performance measures and standards from the time they were adopted until the present?)

- Effects of measures and standards (For example, what changes have occurred in program evaluation procedures as a result of measures and standards?)

- Technical assistance and support for measures and standards (For example, what technical assistance has been provided by the state? By the district?).

Copies of our interview protocols can be found in the appendixes.

DATA ANALYSIS

We compiled extensive notes in the course of our interviews, which we then edited, summarized, and distributed to all members of the research team. Impressions gained in initial visits to the states were tested during subsequent visits, and respondent comments were compared across institutions. The findings documented in this report represent the results of many discussions and formal meetings during which we attempted to synthesize what we had collectively observed over the span of several weeks in the field.

Chapter Three

WHAT WE FOUND

We begin this chapter with brief summaries of the status and most salient elements of each state's implementation of Perkins II. It is impossible to convey the full complexity of each state's system in such short summaries; however, we have tried to provide enough information to help the reader distinguish among the states and to introduce distinct characteristics of each state's approach.

Following that, we summarize the overall progress these states made in implementing statewide systems of performance measures and standards and compare some of their choices. We also found considerable variation in the way the four states responded to the Perkins II mandates—they followed different procedures, selected different measures and standards, and implemented their systems in different ways—and this variation is discussed next. The section concludes with observations about how much remains to be done, even in these four selected states.

STATE SUMMARIES

We refer to the four states by the pseudonyms Alcorn, Columbia, Erie, and Piedmont. This convention serves both to protect the anonymity of our sources and to preclude interpretations based on existing attitudes toward particular jurisdictions. Most states created two distinct systems—one at the secondary level and another at the postsecondary level—so summaries differentiate between secondary and postsecondary vocational institutions.

Alcorn

Alcorn is a predominantly urban state with a large agricultural sector. It has a major metropolitan area that dominates the economy of the state. At the secondary level, there is an extensive accountability system that includes academic skill exams, a performance-based quality review process on the academic side, and schoolwide report cards. The state hopes to incorporate performance measures and standards into this "academic" accountability system.

Alcorn is in the process of creating a workforce preparation system that will include ten measures and standards at both the secondary and postsecondary levels. This system includes piloting of workplace readiness instruments and the development of industry skill standards and certification. The primary goal of performance measures and standards in Alcorn is to produce high-quality data that can be used to compare the progress of programs across the state. The state made early strides in meeting this goal because of its existing computing capacity and centralized approach. There was evidence of interagency coordination to obtain access to new outcomes data and devotion of staff time to develop a strong data system. However, the complexity and centralized nature of the state's data system have resulted in the delayed dissemination of data to districts. Little attention has been paid to local implementation, particularly how instructors might use the data to improve programs.

At the postsecondary level, the regional accreditation body leads the main accountability initiative. This accreditation effort is moving toward requiring postsecondary institutions to include outcome-based measures. Several other initiatives are pushing community colleges in this direction. Alcorn proposes to establish an "institutional guarantee" in which postsecondary institutions guarantee employers that students have acquired certain occupational skills. The state would like to develop a system that will link accreditation, the state-led program review, and performance measures and standards while also using work-readiness assessment instruments and industry skill standards.

As with the secondary level, however, there has been little evidence that Perkins II performance data have been used by deans and instructors for program improvement purposes. Both deans and regional directors reported that the scope of the data they received was overwhelming and that a strategic targeting of the most relevant data would be necessary to make it useful for improving programs.

Columbia

Columbia is a historically agricultural state with a growing industrial base and expanding school system. Educational accountability has been a major concern of the state legislature for the past decade. Annual school report cards that focus on outcomes are issued for each district and postsecondary institution. Poor performance affects a small part of the pool of funds available for teacher salaries. This accountability system put the state a step ahead in terms of implementing Perkins II measures and standards.

At the secondary level, Columbia has a strong central educational bureaucracy. Schools report data to the state at the student level, which the state analyzes and uses to produce required reports. After reviewing existing data-collection efforts, Columbia adopted eight centralized measures; data for three of the measures were already being collected. The vocational education coordinator is an effective leader who involved staff across the state and created a vision for program improvement. Under her direction, the state moved aggressively to expand a computerized test bank and instructional management system to cover all its vocational courses. This system was developed in anticipation of changes in federal vocational education, and funds from Perkins II were used to transform it into a testing system to provide required occupational measures.

Postsecondary education in Columbia is more decentralized, with institutions retaining considerable autonomy. For example, although they have to produce report cards, each institution collects and analyzes its own data. The vocational education coordinator respects this autonomy and tries to shield the institutions by reducing the "burden" of federal requirements. The state relied on existing measures to form the backbone of its postsecondary Perkins II statewide system.

Erie

Erie is primarily a rural state with a growing student and minority population. Elementary and secondary enrollments increased over 10 percent from 1980 to 1992, and postsecondary enrollments grew over 25 percent from 1987 to 1991. Accountability is important in Erie—recent state legislation requires standardized assessment in several grades. At the same time, school districts have a long history of autonomy and retain a great deal of independence. Coordinating state and federal legislation, in conjunction with wide local discretion, has been difficult for the state in its efforts to implement the Perkins II measures and standards. Additionally, unclear communication at the local level has confused local agencies about performance measures and standards.

Having a single state department that is responsible for both secondary and postsecondary occupational education eased the process of selecting measures and standards for Erie. The state adopted a total of nine measures—six based on data that the state was already collecting. The other three were defined conceptually by the state but were passed to the local agencies to operationalize and implement. These three are to be measures of academic and occupational achievement—perhaps the most difficult to operationalize and implement with local resources.

Staffing changes at the state level also resulted in a short hiatus in contact between the state and local agencies. As a result, the local secondary and postsecondary agencies we interviewed have largely ignored the six measures and standards the state was already collecting and have been perplexed with the three that they were given to operationalize. The state and local agencies could be best described as "regrouping" in their efforts to implement the measures and standards. The state is reconsidering the set of measures and standards it selected, and local secondary and postsecondary agencies are beginning to struggle with operationalizing and implementing the three measures and standards that are their responsibility.

Piedmont

Piedmont is a predominantly urban state with a growing and increasingly diverse population. Its major metropolitan area has grown dramatically in the last decade and has become the regional hub for business and financial services.   Perkins performance measures and standards represent the main accountability initiative for vocational education in Piedmont at the secondary level. Traditionally, local agencies have enjoyed autonomy, with the state's role primarily limited to compliance monitoring.   However, with the implementation of performance measures and standards, the state's role has dramatically shifted from monitoring compliance to providing technical assistance to foster program improvement. The state adopted four outcome areas and standards; each district chose or developed its own assessment instruments to evaluate students in these areas.   Vocational teachers have played an active role in developing pre- and post-tests to measure related academic gain and competency attainment. This has encouraged vocational teachers to think about the academic skills related to the occupational competencies they teach. The state developed an extensive technical assistance program for local districts, including a detailed guide to collecting Perkins-related data and a series of regional workshops for vocational education directors.

At the postsecondary level, Piedmont is even more decentralized, with each institution having considerable autonomy. The vocational education coordinator respects the autonomy of each institution and in general has tried to minimize the data burden on vocational deans and instructors. At the postsecondary level Piedmont adopted a scaled-down version of the secondary performance measures and standards—most of the system to be phased in slowly. The main accountability initiative at this level has not come from the state but from the regional accreditation body. To minimize the data-gathering burden, the state originally decided to use the same cohort of students that the federal student right-to-know legislation requires.[1] However, this cohort proved to be too limited and not useful for the purpose of improving programs. The vocational deans plan to expand the cohort this year. Because of the limited cohort and the importance placed on the accreditation system, there has been little ev-

---

[1]The Student Right-to-Know and Campus Security Act, P.L. 101-542, November 8, 1990, requires postsecondary institutions to collect and publish data on the completion or graduation rate of certificate or degree-seeking full-time students. Regulations implementing this act were still pending in 1994.

idence that performance measures and standards have been widely adopted and used for program improvement purposes. There is a perception among some faculty members that performance measures and standards represent another superfluous federal "add-on" program.

IMPLEMENTATION PROGRESS TO DATE

We selected these four states for this study, because they were among the "early adopters" of measures and standards and had made considerable progress in implementing their statewide systems at the time of the study. The committees of practitioners in all four states had formally adopted the measures and standards; to the best of our knowledge, all four states were in compliance with the Perkins II regulations. On average, these states had adopted seven outcomes at the secondary level and nine outcomes at the postsecondary level. Table 3.1 shows the breadth of the measures adopted at the secondary level. All four states adopted measures of academic skills, specific occupational competencies, and labor-market outcomes. Most also had measures of general job or work skills and of program retention and/or completion. The pattern was similar at the secondary level. Table 3.2 shows that three of the four states adopted postsecondary measures in the majority of these major outcome areas.

Some of the states were phasing in one or more elements of their systems over a one- or two-year period, but the vast majority of the components were fully operational in the 1993–94 school year. Data were collected during that year for most measures, although analysis and reporting of these data will not occur until the 1994–95 school year in many cases.

In addition to the measures described in Tables 3.1 and 3.2, all four states either had or were actively developing the necessary information infrastructure to support standards-based accountability. Columbia and Erie have computerized student recordkeeping systems in place that could be used for analyzing and reporting progress toward state standards and functioning paper-based data systems for collecting most of the remainder of the statewide measures. Alcorn was expanding its existing centralized data-collection and analysis system to accommodate newly adopted measures, while Piedmont

Table 3.1

Secondary Measures in Four States

Outcome	Alcorn	Columbia	Erie	Piedmont
Academic skills	Attainment on state test of academic skills	Gains[a] on state test of literacy[b]	Attainment on locally selected tests of foundation skills[b]	Gains[a] on locally selected tests of academic skills
Specific occupational competencies	Attainment on state test of technical skills and applied academics[b]	Attainment and gains[a] on test of core occupational competencies	Attainment on locally selected measures of occupational competencies[b]	Attainment of locally selected course competencies
General job or work skills	Attainment on state test of workplace skills[b]	Attainment and gains[a] on test of work skills	Attainment of workplace competencies[b]	N/A[c]
Retention or completion	Percentage of students completing program and graduating	N/A[c]	Increase in program completion and graduation	School completion rate of enrolled students
Labor market	Percentage of completers employed in related field or in further education or training	Percentage of completers employed in related fields or in further education or training	Increase in percentage of completers employed in related fields or in further education or training	Percentage of completers employed in related field or in further education or training
Other	Employment retention	Comparison to county unemployment rate; career development planning		

[a]Measured as the difference between posttest and pretest scores.
[b]Under development.
[c]N/A reflects an outcome not chosen by the state.

Table 3.2

Postsecondary Measures in Four States

Outcome	Alcorn	Columbia	Erie	Piedmont
Academic skills	Completion of remedial courses	Completion of general education, related and remedial courses	Attainment on locally selected tests of foundation skills[a]	Completion of academic courses
Specific occupational competencies	Attainment on state test of technical skills and applied academics[a]	N/A[b]	Attainment on locally selected measures of occupational competencies[a]	Completion of occupational programs
General job or work skills	Attainment on state test of workplace skills[a]	N/A[b]	Attainment of workplace competencies[a]	N/A[b]
Retention or completion	Percentage of students completing program	Percentage of required credit hours completed, course sequence completed, reenrollment rate	Increase in program completion and persistence	N/A[b]
Labor market	Percentage of completers employed in related field or in further education or training	N/A[b]	Increase in percentage of completers employed in related field or in further education or training	Percentage of completers employed in related field or in further education or training
Other	Employment retention			

[a]Under development.
[b]N/A reflects an outcome not chosen by the state.

was devoting considerable resources to developing local capacity for data collection and analysis consistent with its decentralized approach to measures and standards.

All four states made efforts to coordinate the implementation of their systems of measures and standards with other state and federal occupational training and economic development programs, as required by the Perkins II guidelines. Unfortunately, the states found very little common ground between the measures and standards developed by vocational educators in response to Perkins II and the data systems in use by other agencies. Although all four states attempted to coordinate data elements among their diverse economic development efforts, none had great success in this effort. Many states were working toward using unemployment insurance wage records as placement data across agencies.

Finally, all four states had begun to prepare local educational agencies for their roles in the standards-based accountability system. A few of the local school or college staff people we interviewed were involved directly in the selection or adoption of measures or standards; they were familiar with the requirements from the outset. The remainder of the local staff had learned about the new requirements subsequently. Almost everyone we spoke to was aware of the measures and standards in general terms if not in specific detail. Three of the four states informed local programs about the data demands and the accountability standards in fairly traditional ways, assigning dissemination and training responsibility to existing state program or area staff, distributing written information, presenting regional workshops, etc. Efforts in the fourth state went well beyond those in the others, perhaps because local programs were responsible for selecting the measurement tools to be used to assess outcomes. In this state, the number of workshops and the amount of contact with local program staff were considerably greater than in the others.

VARIATIONS IN IMPLEMENTATION

One of the most striking findings from our interviews and observations was the large degree of variation in the way each of the four states implemented Perkins II requirements. States' approaches to Perkins II measures and standards differed in almost every respect, including who participated in the process, how the process was managed, what resources were devoted to it, how the regulations were interpreted, and how the system was integrated with existing state and local initiatives.

The inherent "flexible" nature of the directive in Perkins II to develop and implement a system of performance measures and standards encouraged states to customize their systems to meet local needs. Moreover, states interpreted the law in different ways, which led to further variation in implementation. For example, states had different interpretations of the requirement to measure learning and competency gains. Some felt that the measurement of "gain" requires pre- and posttest scores; others chose to use course completion as a proxy for improvement. In the absence of strong federal control over interpretation, states acted in the spirit of "flexibility," creating their own interpretations. In the next chapter, we attempt to describe some of the factors that affected states' interpretations and responses to Perkins II.

Implementation at the postsecondary level is moving more slowly and is more varied than at the secondary level. This difference in implementation is due largely to the historical autonomy granted to postsecondary institutions. The movement toward educational accountability has only recently come to the postsecondary level, and there it faces unique challenges. For example, except for the purposes of initial placement, postsecondary institutions do not use assessment systems to test the achievement of students. Lacking basic achievement measures, it is almost impossible to measure learning "gain." A second factor in slowing the implementation of Perkins II at the postsecondary level is the diversity of student purposes that postsecondary institutions must serve. It is difficult to establish a system to track the progress of community college students with different purposes for attending schools. An "entering" class will include eighteen year olds out of high school, adult workers who need one course to upgrade their skills, and unemployed people who need retraining.

ROOM FOR IMPROVEMENT

Although these four states were among the leaders in implementing Perkins II measures and standards, their systems were only partially complete at the time of this study. No state had yet completed a full cycle of data collection, analysis, and reporting on all adopted measures, and no local program had yet examined its own performance in light of statewide standards as a guide to program improvement.

Additionally, many states still had proposed measurement tools under development. Columbia proposed to measure literacy in terms of pretest to posttest gains, but had not yet taken any steps to develop a literacy assessment instrument. Common unresolved testing or assessment problems included the measurement of academic and occupational skills and difficulty setting up systems to monitor the performance of special populations.

Most states' efforts were focused on creating statewide systems that would be in compliance with the federal regulations; much less thought had been given to the use of the data the system produced for program improvement. Moreover, both state and local agencies had done little to translate information on program status into actions for program improvement. We saw only one or two instances in which thought had been given to converting standards-based reports into action plans.

Finally, with the exception of one highly decentralized state, most state departments of education were only beginning to provide extensive information and training to local program staff. By the spring of 1994, states had disseminated to local districts the new rules and data requirements introduced by the statewide system. States were just beginning to confront the need for more local staff development, for greater contact with programs as they prepared new annual applications, and for linking accountability with program improvement.

The states in our study have made a good start in implementing their systems of measures and standards, as envisioned in Perkins II. However, conditions at all levels of government have resulted in some states making greater progress than others. In the next chapter, we attempt to explain why variations in progress have occurred.

Chapter Four

WHAT EXPLAINS PROGRESS TO DATE?

We identified a number of factors that contributed to the observed similarities and differences in states' implementation of Perkins II systems of measures and standards. Some of these explanatory factors are within the sphere of influence of federal policy; others are within the domains of states and local agencies. In Chapter Five, we will draw upon the federal factors we discuss in this chapter to make recommendations for changes in federal policy to improve the implementation of Perkins II.

FACTORS SUBJECT TO FEDERAL INFLUENCE

The first set of factors we identified includes elements of the 1990 Perkins legislation and other conditions that may be directly influenced by federal policy. These factors include the following:

- Flexibility provided to the states in the law itself

- Unclear integration and coordination of Perkins II provisions

- Lack of models or incentives for state and local implementation

- Limited expertise and resources at the state level

- Mandated measurement of learning outcomes.

Modifying these features through legislative or administrative means may enhance future implementation of Perkins II measures and standards in the states. We discuss each of these factors in greater detail below.

Flexibility Provided to the States in the Law

The framers of the legislation sought to impose a common outcome-oriented program-improvement framework. They also wanted to enact policy that was sensitive to state differences and that permitted local adaptation, which research suggests should foster implementation (Berman and McLaughlin, 1978). As a result, Perkins II gave states considerable latitude in choosing measures, setting standards, deciding how much responsibility to delegate to local districts and institutions, and designing program-improvement interventions. This flexibility permitted states to create systems that were responsive to local conditions but also increased the influence of contextual factors, which had both positive and negative effects.

On the positive side, the flexible mandate engaged states actively in developing their systems of measures and standards, gave states the opportunity to develop a sense of ownership, and enabled states to adapt the accountability system to their existing program review and monitoring efforts, potentially reducing costly duplication of effort. Furthermore, Perkins II gave states complete control over the nature of state assistance to failing programs, so these efforts could be aligned with ongoing program review and improvement activities. On the negative side, flexibility has increased the influence of local context on the structure of the accountability system, reducing the comparability of state systems and program results. The act provided little guidance about the nature of the relationship that state agencies and local programs were to have in these new systems or about the state's role in providing technical assistance to local programs. Some states have done little or nothing to elaborate this relationship or build effective technical assistance procedures. In these cases, state discretion led to decisions that might not be considered to be in the spirit of the legislation or in the best interests of program improvement.

The overall result of the legislative flexibility is mixed. In 1994, we found little evidence that states had created a dynamic program-improvement culture based on outcome data, which many believe to be the intent of Perkins II. Furthermore, it appears to us that openness in the law, combined with strong state contextual factors, has lengthened substantially the timeframe for development and implementation. Even states that are moving in the right direction are moving more slowly than envisioned in the legislation.

Unclear Integration and Coordination of Perkins II Provisions

Although Perkins II appears to emphasize measures and standards, service to special populations, integrating academic and vocational curricula, and tech-prep education[1] equally, state agencies treated these as separate requirements and assigned them different priorities. The four states we visited differed in the emphasis they placed on developing and implementing performance measures and standards relative to the other Perkins II initiatives. These differences in state priorities accounted for some of the differences we observed in progress toward systems of measures and standards.

Similarly, Perkins II is unclear about how performance measures and standards are to be used to evaluate its other new priorities—service to special populations, tech-prep education, and the integration of academic and vocational education. Perkins II offers little guidance about how any of these activities are to be coordinated. Furthermore, by giving states nearly two years to develop their performance measures and standards systems, Perkins II makes coordination more difficult.[2] While state administrators were developing systems of measures and standards, state and local administrators were beginning to implement tech-prep education programs and integration strategies. The two-year development phase for performance measures and standards inhibited the use of these systems as evaluation tools for the other Perkins initiatives.

---

[1]"The term 'tech-prep education program' means a combined secondary and postsecondary program which leads to an associate degree or 2-year certificate; provides technical preparation in at least 1 field of engineering technology, applied science, mechanical, industrial, or practical art or trade, or agriculture, health, or business; builds student competence in mathematics, science, and communications (including through applied academics) through a sequential course of study; and leads to placement in employment." (The Carl D. Perkins Vocational and Applied Technology Education Act Amendments of 1990. P.L. 101–392; Part E, Sec. 347.)

[2]According to Rahn and Alt (1994), 45 states reported an increase in the amount of time spent developing performance measures and standards from 1990 to 1993 at the secondary education level. At the postsecondary level, 41 states reported an increase in time spent in this area.

Ideally, each state's system of performance measures and standards would be used to assess the effectiveness of vocational programs, including the performance of special populations, tech-prep education students, and students in programs with integrated academic and vocational curricula. In fact, Erie included specific language in its measures and standards to require their application to special populations. One can imagine an ideal accountability system that provides information on the performance of tech-prep education students, youth apprenticeship students, and each special subpopulation in a program. With such data, a local administrator would be able to compare the performance of subpopulations within a program, compare vocational programs within a school, and compare a particular program to overall school performance. Moreover, this system would facilitate coordination between academic and vocational teachers, by providing measures of relevant academic and vocational skills on each student. Most importantly, comparative program information would allow administrators and instructors to target program-improvement strategies. For example, if the tech-prep education program consistently exceeded all standards, an administrator might try to transform more vocational programs into tech-prep education programs.

Unfortunately, the Perkins II priorities—measures and standards, service to special populations, integrating academic and vocational curricula, tech-prep education—are treated like disjointed programs, uncoordinated and at a different stage of implementation. In most states, Perkins II priorities are not part of a coordinated system at either the state or the local level, and performance measures and standards are not being used comprehensively to evaluate the other Perkins II initiatives.

Lack of Models or Incentives for State and Local Implementation

There is a major gap between development of measures and standards (which usually occurred at the state level) and implementation of standards-based program-improvement systems (which must occur at the local level). Development dominated state agency efforts in the four states we visited. Certainly, it is necessary to select measures and standards and to create data systems to support them before these systems can be implemented. However, some state agencies had devoted so much attention to development that they had barely thought about subsequent stages of reform, such as how local administrators and instructors would use performance measures and standards to improve programs.

The situation in one state reminded a researcher of the void that occurred following the birth of his first child. All of his and his wife's attention had been focused on the delivery (for instance, on childbirth classes and exercises) with little or no thought to what would come after. Once the child was born, it came as a sudden shock to the parents that they now had to care for the child on a daily basis. It appeared that some states were in a similar position vis-à-vis Perkins II performance measures and standards. They focused extensively on the "birth" of measures and standards, but they devoted little time to thinking about implementing them or using them once they were created. States were unprepared for the next step, because the demands of the development stage overshadowed concerns about implementation.

This shortsightedness may have occurred because Perkins II modeled a two-stage reform but did not provide two stages of incentives. The Office of Vocational and Adult Education monitored the submission of state plans and the adoption of measures and standards, but there were no incentives for ensuring that performance measures and standards would be used at the local level to improve programs. Furthermore, while programs that did not make substantial progress toward the state standards for two years were required to develop a local improvement plan in conjunction with the state, there were no other explicit mechanisms in the law for monitoring local use of the measures and standards.

For example, Erie adopted nine measures and standards (six of which were based on data that were already being collected). Local agencies were required to select or develop measurement tools for the three new outcome areas. However, local administrators received no training in how to select appropriate instruments and have had very little contact from the state to see whether they were taking appropriate actions. Furthermore, the state has shown no interest in knowing whether they were using the measures and standards for program improvement. One postsecondary site responded by initiating a campuswide effort to develop new measures, but another did almost nothing. With very little guidance from the state, local implementation depended almost entirely on individual initiative at the local level.

Despite the lack of models or incentives provided in the legislation, one state agency succeeded in promoting the use of performance measures and standards at the local level, in part because the state administrator believed in the usefulness of performance data for local program improvement and seized the opportunity to implement such a system. The secondary vocational education agency in Piedmont adopted an approach in which local programs chose measures from among several outcome areas and selected their own specific measurement tools. Furthermore, the state agency provided training, developed guidebooks and report formats, and took other steps to make the local programs feel that their participation was important. Although the state agency did not offer rewards or levy penalties, it created an atmosphere that fostered local participation and, ultimately, implementation.

Limited Expertise and Resources at the State Level

The Perkins II performance measures and standards mandate created new responsibilities for state staff, requiring them to develop expertise in new and often unfamiliar areas. At the same time, the act also reduced the set-aside for state administration, to put more resources into direct services. This left some states in a bind: They lacked both the expertise to address new demands and the resources needed to develop it.

Vocational education agencies in these four states differed in the numbers of staff members; the sizes of their administrative budgets; the levels of expertise in the areas of psychometrics, statistics, and labor-market economics; and their capacities to implement local reforms. In Erie, a single individual was responsible for statewide implementation at the secondary and postsecondary levels, in addition to other duties. This severely limited the time and energy that could be devoted to performance measures and standards. In other cases, staff did not possess the expertise needed to develop a program-improvement system based on outcome data. For example, one state director commented, "My staff are in over their heads. There is not one trained research person on staff. We wanted initially to conduct a labor market analysis, but we just didn't have anyone who knew how to do it."

Some state agencies made performance measures and standards a high enough priority to allocate staff and funds to the effort; others devoted only limited resources to this area. Moreover, most states focused the bulk of their resources on developing their systems of measures and standards. Staff in some state education agencies complained about not having enough funds to provide the technical assistance necessary to implement performance measures and standards effectively. Our site visits revealed a continuing need for additional staff training in using outcome data for program improvement and a growing demand for technical assistance in this area.

Mandated Measurement of Learning Outcomes

Perkins II requires states to measure academic learning gain and suggests that states adopt measures of job or work skill and competency attainment as well. The scarcity of valid assessment tools in these areas led states to adopt alternatives that were less than optimal. For example, some states delayed or phased in their performance measures and standards, because these states lacked measurement tools in some areas. All four states we visited lacked one or more measurement tools needed to complete their systems. Some states assumed the responsibility for developing new instruments, while other states selected from among measurement tools that were available. All were deficient in some manner. Still other states chose from among available instruments but recognized their shortcomings and planned to revisit the choices in the future. In addition, the act does not include definitions for key terms, such as "basic" and "more advanced" academic skills, which has led to widely varying interpretations and approaches. As one state director put it, the performance measures and standards mandate is "putting the cart before the horse." He would prefer developing industry skill standards first, then appropriate assessments, and only last a system of measures and standards.

Alcorn and Columbia used standardized tests of academic achievement at the secondary level to measure basic academic skills. These tests have been criticized, because they do not measure the academic skills for which vocational programs should be held account-able and do not measure these skills in a manner suitable for voca-tional students. To address some of these concerns, one state was developing an academic assessment instrument specifically de-signed for vocational students.

In Erie and Piedmont, state agencies delegated to local agencies the responsibility for selecting and/or developing academic assess-ments. This decentralized approach defers difficult decisions to local programs, which are less likely to have the expertise required to tackle difficult measurement problems. This strategy raises concerns about the appropriateness of locally selected tests and the technical quality of locally developed measures. Decentralization of mea-surement choices also precludes the direct comparison of program performance.

None of the states in our study possessed statewide academic tests at the postsecondary level. The only postsecondary academic tests in these states were those used to place students into appropriate English and math courses at the time of enrollment. Piedmont and Erie delegated responsibility for selecting or developing measures of postsecondary academic skills to local institutions. The remaining two states used remedial course completion as a proxy for basic aca-demic gain. One used general education and related academic course completion as a proxy for advanced academic gain. In both cases, it was assumed that students who received a passing grade in a course had gained the skills and knowledge covered by the course.[3]

Course completion has been criticized as a measure of academic gains, because it does not directly compare student achievement be-tween separate times. Furthermore, institutions usually define "successful course completion" as receiving a final grade of D or better. None of the instructors interviewed believed that a student who received a D could have mastered the body of knowledge con-tained in a course. Another criticism of measures of course comple-tion relates to remedial courses. Some instructors felt it was inap-propriate to hold vocational programs accountable for student gains

---

[3]In a nationwide survey, more than one-third of all states at the postsecondary level reported using course completion as a proxy for academic gain (Rahn, Hoachlander, and Levesque, 1993).

in preprogram, remedial courses, while others noted that it was wrong to credit vocational programs for academic gains that occur in these courses prior to enrollment in a vocational program.

FACTORS SUBJECT TO STATE AND LOCAL INFLUENCE

The second set of factors affecting successful implementation of the Perkins II system of measures and standards flows from the contexts of individual states and localities. As a result, these factors are primarily responsive to state or local action. Without state or local action, the following factors may continue to exercise a dampening effect on the results of federal policy:

- Choice between central and local implementation strategies

- Existence of centralized data systems

- Availability of state-level assessment tools

- Ongoing educational accountability and program review mechanisms

- Historical relationships among agencies

- Efforts to reduce burdens on local program staff

- Influence of key administrators.

State responses to the Perkins II accountability initiatives have been influenced by local factors; some of these advanced the development and/or implementation of state performance measures and standards systems and others impeded it.

Choice Between Central and Local Implementation Strategy

A key factor that contributed to differences in state implementation is the division of responsibility between state and local agencies for developing and implementing measures and standards. Centralized approaches tended to be more efficient in the short term, but decentralized ones may have greater long-term potential for local program improvement.

In this study, state vocational education agencies with a history of centralized decisionmaking selected outcome areas, stipulated specific measurement tools, set standards, and identified criteria that would trigger local improvement plans. In contrast, states with a history of strong local control tended to confine their roles to selecting general measurement areas and defining broad standards. Local educational agencies and postsecondary institutions were given responsibility for selecting specific measurment instruments and for deciding whether their institution was making sufficient progress toward meeting state standards. In some cases, the approach to performance measures and standards differed at the secondary and postsecondary levels in the same state.

To illustrate, in Alcorn, the state staff (with input from the committee of practitioners) selected measurement areas, developed instruments, and established overall state standards and aggregate performance goals for the whole system. For example, academic achievement at the secondary level was to be measured using a standardized statewide test, and employment outcomes at both the secondary and postsecondary levels were to be measured using state unemployment insurance data during particular quarters following program completion. In a similar vein, Columbia required local recipients either to use state-developed measurement tools or to use state-defined methods of calculating performance on locally chosen measures.

In contrast, Piedmont and Erie, with stronger traditions of local control, delegated responsibility for developing or selecting some or all measurement instruments to local recipients. (Standards were set centrally in these two states.) In Piedmont, local school districts were allowed to develop their own academic and occupational competencies and measurement instruments or to adopt state-developed ones, while districts were required to administer their own program follow-up surveys. In the four states we examined, where local agencies were responsible for development and/or implementation of some measures and standards, more delays, confusion, and technical problems occurred than in states where these decisions were made centrally.

Although systems with increased local responsibility faced early difficulties, one state may be poised to achieve greater success because of the investments the state made in local expertise. In contrast, the early successes of systems with more centralized control may diminish if steps are not taken to engage local administrators in the program improvement process. For example, the data generated by the centralized performance measures and standards system in Alcorn were rarely being used by instructors to improve their course offerings. Although some district and institution administrators were using the data to identify broad problem areas, instructors stated that the data were too voluminous, complicated, and general to provide them with the information they needed and desired to improve their programs. Rather than numerous pages of tabular data, instructors preferred a simplified presentation format, and rather than an overall employment rate for program completers, they desired information on the specific employers who had hired their completers, on the specific jobs those completers had taken, and on the skills they were using or needed in those jobs. Furthermore, several administrators had not yet passed the performance measures and standards data on to their instructors, believing the instructors would be overwhelmed, and some spoke candidly that they did not expect their instructors ever to use the data.

In contrast, at the secondary level in Piedmont, the highly decentralized performance measures and standards system led to widespread use by instructors of related academic assessments and the performance data generated by them. Because these assessments had been developed locally with support and encouragement from the state, instructors found them relevant for assessing student outcomes and improving programs. Furthermore, instructors and administrators found the performance report formats supplied by the state useful and understandable.

These examples illustrate strong differences in local use of performance measures and standards related to the degree of centralized or decentralized development, but the differences are not always so great. A centralized approach may be more efficient, may lead to more elaborate and well-organized data, and may provide greater interprogram comparability. A decentralized approach may help ensure that performance measures and standards are relevant locally and may lead to greater local participation in and commitment to the program review and improvement process.

Existence of Centralized Data Systems

Statewide student databases and data-processing capabilities affected state responses to Perkins II performance measures and standards initiatives. Agencies with centralized data systems were more likely to assume a strong role in collecting and reporting performance measures and standards than those without such systems. Although this is not always true, states with more centralized record-keeping experience and the computer capacity to maintain and analyze large-scale databases were more likely to construct centralized data systems in response to Perkins II.

For example, in Alcorn and Columbia, the state vocational education agencies obtained data for some performance measures from other educational departments or state agencies, compiled those data, and reported them to local school districts and community colleges. For other measurement areas, local administrators reported data to the state vocational education agency, which then summarized performance on the measures and standards and returned the data to their originators in a revised form. In both cases, the state vocational education agencies played an important role in either collecting or reporting the data. As a consequence, even though many of the data were locally generated, administrators and instructors in these states viewed performance measures and standards data as belonging to the state. One postsecondary dean said, "The data don't match ours, but this lets us know how the state views us."

In contrast, at the secondary level in Piedmont, the state vocational education agency played only a minimal role in data collection and reporting. Local school districts compiled their own data, tallied the appropriate statistics, and reported them to the state agency on standard report forms that had been supplied by the state. Local administrators and instructors we interviewed in this state were more knowledgeable about and interested in the performance measures and standards than local staff in other states.

A second consequence of a centralized data system is that it contributed to states focusing on the data more than how the data could be used. For example, Alcorn's data-computing capacity led state-level vocational education staff and the committee of practitioners to envision a sophisticated system of performance measures and standards that would provide local school districts and community colleges with a broad range of outcome data at many levels of aggregation, including district, school or institution, program, and special populations' status. However, while devoting substantial time to developing this data system, state staff spent less time thinking through how the data would be used at the local level to improve programs. As one state-level administrator stated, "We've provided them with all the data; now all they need to do is use it." Although the system succeeded in generating hundreds of pages of data per school or community college district, there was little evidence that the data were being used at the local level, particularly by instructors. At the end of the second year of implementation of performance measures and standards, state-level staff still placed a higher priority on improving data quality than on improving local use for program evaluation and improvement.

In contrast, secondary-level state staff in Piedmont had minimal capacity to collect and manipulate data. They devoted their time to developing guidelines for local agencies to follow and to providing other technical assistance to support local development efforts.

Availability of State-Level Assessment Tools

As noted above, certain provisions of Perkins II create assessment problems for all states—for example, the requirement that state systems include measures of academic learning gains has been a universal stumbling block—and it is appropriate for the federal government to take steps to address these concerns. However, other aspects of assessment affect the implementation of measures and standards at the state and local levels in ways that may not be addressed best by federal action. In particular, the interplay between a state's choice of measures and standards and the state's existing testing system affects the implementation of the measures and standards. Furthermore, states that delegated decisions about vocational measures to local agencies added another layer of sensitivity to state and local assessment experience and practice.

States' actions in implementing measures and standards were affected by the prior existence of relevant state assessment tools. Where such measurement tools existed, states generally incorporated them into their performance measures and standards systems, although the use of existing measures had mixed results. For example, Columbia and Alcorn relied on existing statewide standardized tests of academic achievement to satisfy the requirement to measure "learning and competency gains, including student progress in the achievement of basic and more advanced academic skills" at the secondary level. These existing academic tests served as readily available measures, but they also had several limitations. For one, tests in both states assessed academic attainment in early high school—neither test had the capacity to measure the gains students achieved throughout their high school years. Both state agencies planned to phase in an additional test to measure gains, but neither had yet done so. Second, these standardized academic tests were not designed to measure academic skills specifically related to occupational competencies, which many vocational educators have argued should be the focus of Perkins II performance measures and standards. Third, instructors do not always find results relevant to their courses. Currently, neither state plans to develop tests of occupationally related academic skills.

In contrast, Piedmont's secondary-level state staff focused on helping instructors develop measures of the relevant academic skills and occupational competencies appropriate for specific local programs. The state also sponsored the development of statewide prototype tests that instructors could choose to implement in lieu of developing their own local tests. Although developing these tests took substantial time and staff resources and although questions of test validity and reliability remain to be addressed, Piedmont's vocational educators were able to produce tests that measured both student gains and related academic skills.

No statewide measure of academic performance existed in Erie, so state staff required local recipients at both the secondary and postsecondary levels to choose or develop appropriate measures of academic and occupational skill gains. Although state staff identified the skills that should be measured in general terms, they provided little assistance to local agencies in selecting appropriate assessments. Some staff questioned whether the instruments that had been selected by some local agencies would adequately assess the intended skills.

At the postsecondary level, none of the states in our study possessed a statewide measure of academic skills. Although Erie required local recipients to seek or develop an appropriate measure, the other three states measured academic gains through course completion. For example, states counted successful completion of developmental or remedial courses or of general education or related academic courses as academic gains. However, state-level staff in Alcorn were developing tests of basic reading and mathematics skills at the postsecondary level.

The lack of relevant instruments for measuring academic and occupational competency led states to adopt alternative strategies for measuring learning outcomes. These alternatives often were not the most appropriate. Furthermore, difficulties in measuring academic and occupational skills forced states to slow implementation of this portion of the Perkins II mandate. In a few cases, Perkins II requirements spurred states to develop their own instruments, which appeared to be suitable at first glance.

Ongoing Educational Accountability and Program Review Mechanisms

States' reactions to Perkins II were strongly influenced by the educational accountability context that existed within the states. Some states had strong accountability mechanisms that attached incentives or sanctions to educational performance, although weaker accountability systems were more common. All states had program review and accreditation procedures designed to monitor and/or certify educational quality. Perkins II measures and standards served a similar purpose, and some states tried to consolidate Perkins II accountability with existing efforts. However, this was not always the case, and it is interesting to explore the degree to which states tried to integrate these activities.

Erie had established an accountability system based on student outcomes for both secondary and postsecondary vocational education several years prior to passage of the act in 1990. In response to Perkins II performance measures and standards requirements, the state added three new measures to the six they had already been collecting. By folding performance measures and standards into an existing accountability system, the state was able to respond quickly to the Perkins II mandates.   It is also possible that by attaching Perkins-specific measures to an established system, local vocational administrators and instructors would be more likely to incorporate them into their local accountability processes.   However, there was little evidence that the existing accountability system was being transformed into the program improvement process envisioned by Perkins.[4]

Alcorn already had several components of an accountability system for elementary and secondary education in place prior to Perkins II. Specifically, the state had been issuing school report cards for a number of years and had recently initiated a review process whereby schools regularly evaluated their performance in state-specified areas based on locally selected measures.   However, neither the report cards nor the review process incorporated outcome measures relevant to vocational education.   While state vocational education staff members have begun a dialogue with general education staff to bring Perkins II efforts closer to other strictly academic accountability efforts, by 1994, performance measures and standards had been developed and implemented largely in isolation from the general accountability initiatives.

Previous experience with statewide school report cards had both positive and negative effects on the development of Perkins II measures and standards in Alcorn.   On one hand, state and local administrators, instructors, and members of the committee of practitioners were already familiar with the idea of using outcome data to evaluate institutional performance, which may have facilitated development of a system of performance measures and standards. On the other hand, this same experience may have led state staff to ignore how the data would realistically be used locally to improve programs.   As an accountability tool, the school report card was used largely by school administrators as "a public relations piece," in the words of one superintendent, primarily in discussions with school

---

[4]Early evidence indicated that, without follow-through and assistance from state staff, local programs were largely ignoring the requirement for new measures.   Because the state had been responsible for collecting the six extant measures and had done little to encourage use of the data, local administrators were paying scant attention to the measures as well.

boards and parents. Instructors paid little attention to these data, because they were not provided in a form useful to them and because they were used to make comparisons between districts the instructors felt were unfair. As with the school report cards, state-level staff passed the performance measures and standards reports down through the secondary and postsecondary education hierarchies, expecting them to reach instructors who would then use the information to improve programs. However, by the end of the second year of implementation of performance measures and standards, few instructors had ever seen the data, and there was widespread skepticism among local administrators that instructors would ever use them.

In addition to these accountability initiatives, states also had other evaluation and program review systems in place prior to Perkins II. Most state vocational education agencies followed a multiyear cyclical program review process at both the secondary and postsecondary levels. State-level vocational education staff indicated that performance measures and standards data would likely be incorporated into the multiyear program review process.

Additionally, all postsecondary institutions were subject to periodic reviews by independent regional accreditation agencies. While the cyclical program reviews traditionally focused on process measures, such as vocational enrollments and sex-equity issues, the regional postsecondary accreditation agencies have recently begun moving toward outcome-based evaluations. Evidence in several states indicated that Perkins II performance measures and standards were taking a back seat to the accreditation process at the postsecondary level, particularly in those institutions that recently went through the new outcome-based accreditation process. In part because accreditation is crucial to the viability of an institution, accreditation requirements were receiving greater attention than Perkins II. Furthermore, the accreditation process is generally well regarded by postsecondary institutions, because it permits them to evaluate themselves in terms of their own goals. In contrast, some feel that Perkins II performance measures and standards are centrally dictated without appropriate institutional contribution. However, since accreditation reviews sometimes occur as infrequently as once every ten years, the annual Perkins requirements may gain in importance over time.

Other federal accountability requirements also influenced states' responses to Perkins II. For example, recent federal student right-to-know legislation requires that postsecondary institutions receiving federal financial aid track the educational experiences of a cohort of full-time students. At least one state in our sample tried to consolidate requirements by using this same cohort in its Perkins II performance measures and standards system. However, because first-time, full-time students are often a minority at community colleges, instructors generally found the performance data they received useless for program improvement. For example, one Piedmont instructor had only three students in the selected cohort (and one of these had been sent to prison). The instructor did not believe that the resulting 33 percent incarcerated outcome rate accurately reflected his program performance and did not find that it provided him with useful information for improving his program.

In summary, the relationship between existing accountability initiatives and development of Perkins II performance measures and standards was complex. Combining these various efforts may ultimately bolster them all. However, Perkins II emphasizes program improvement, while many of the other initiatives do not. This emphasis may be lost if Perkins II accountability is joined with systems that use performance data for other purposes. Furthermore, where federal regulatory demands are in conflict, practical constraints may force states to satisfy one requirement at the expense of another.

Historical Relationships Among Agencies

Existing governance structures and collaboration patterns among state agencies affected states' responses to Perkins II requirements. For example, unified secondary and postsecondary vocational education agencies or agencies that were housed in the same state office produced coordinated Perkins II efforts: Erie agencies adopted a single set of performance measures and standards for both levels of education, while Alcorn agencies adopted parallel sets of measures and standards and worked together to develop new outcome data. In contrast, Columbia secondary and postsecondary vocational education agencies historically acted separately, and they developed wholly different and separate performance measures and standards systems. In Piedmont, the secondary vocational education agency took the lead in developing its performance measures and standards system, after which the postsecondary agency scaled down the secondary system for its own implementation.

In addition to historical relationships between secondary and postsecondary vocational education agencies, responses to Perkins II requirements were also affected by existing relationships between these agencies and those responsible for general education, the Job Training Partnership Act (JTPA), and other workforce programs. For example, the Alcorn state vocational education agency operated largely separately from the elementary and secondary education agency and the community college board. They had to establish formal links to obtain data from these agencies, a process that was facilitated because of historically good relations among them. In some cases, the federal performance measures and standards initiative provoked new inter-agency collaboration. For example, the Perkins emphasis on placement outcomes spurred the Alcorn vocational education agency to collaborate with the state's JTPA agency, which had substantial experience using state unemployment insurance data for obtaining employment and earnings outcomes.

Efforts to Reduce Burden on Local Administrators

Reducing the data-collection and reporting burden on local administrators was foremost in the minds of many state vocational education agencies when they designed their systems of measures and standards. This approach appeared to expedite the selection of performance measures and standards and the collection and reporting of data and to increase initial acceptance of performance measures and standards by local administrators. However, efforts to reduce the burden of measures and standards may also reduce the effectiveness of the system in the long run by limiting local familiarity and "buy-in." Moreover, the focus on burden reflects a narrow perception of the system of measures and standards as a reporting exercise, not as an essential core activity in a meaningful program management and improvement system.

Three of the four states we visited attempted to design their measures and standards to minimize data-collection demands on local institutions. In Columbia, state staff at the postsecondary level "made every effort" to adopt measures for which data were already being collected by local institutions. In Erie, six of nine measures adopted were already being collected. Similarly, Alcorn, adopted measures for which local schools already collected data or measures that could be satisfied by data obtained through another state agency. All were proud of these actions, and felt they expedited the process of developing their state systems of measures and standards.

On the other hand, reducing the burden of data collection and reporting also reduced local awareness of the reforms, particularly for instructors. Well into the second year of implementation of Perkins II measures and standards, few instructors in Columbia, Erie, and Alcorn had either heard of performance measures and standards or understood what their role was to be in using them. Furthermore, in at least one case in which performance measures and standards data had been fed back to administrators or instructors, few found the data relevant or felt committed to using them.

In sharp contrast, high school instructors in the sites we visited in Piedmont responded well to the "burden" that was placed on them to develop and implement local assessments of related academic skills and occupational competencies. While some local personnel initially resisted the new requirements, most became more positive with time and with continued encouragement and support from the state. In this case, local educators who were invited to participate in the process and now have greater ownership over the results responded well to the additional responsibilities placed on them by federal or state mandates. Furthermore, local educators who were involved in data definition, instrument development, and the like were in a better position to use the data when they were produced. Protecting local educators from the burden of developing a new system may ultimately lessen their capabilities and incentives to use them.

Influence of Key Administrators

The presence or absence of strong leadership affected the nature of states' responses to Perkins II and the progress states made in developing and implementing performance measures and standards. In most of the states, a single individual had primary responsibility for the implementation of performance measures and standards at the secondary or postsecondary level (or both). The commitment of and approach used by this key administrator largely determined the progress made by the state. At one extreme, some key state vocational education staff acted decisively to develop expanded systems. For example, a key administrator in Columbia took advantage of Perkins II mandates to promote reforms she had long wanted to implement. At the other extreme, some key administrators took only those few steps that were necessary for compliance with the law.

These four states revealed dramatic contrasts in the speed and effectiveness with which administrators implemented their statewide systems. Sometimes, secondary and postsecondary systems within the same state varied dramatically. For example, the primary state-level administrator for secondary vocational education in one state was an active and effective change agent who seized upon the Perkins II mandate as an opportunity to promote greater local accountability, a cause in which he believed strongly. He supplied a vision of how the reform would work, rallied enthusiasm for it, and provided support to those who were responsible for enacting the changes. In contrast, the administrator for postsecondary vocational education in the same state did very little to encourage local implementation, stating candidly that he expected the performance measures and standards requirements to go the way of many national initiatives and be forgotten within a few years.

In another state, the vocational coordinator took the performance measures and standards mandate seriously, but kept his role to a minimum. This key administrator communicated with local staff about Perkins II requirements primarily in writing, assuming that school-level staff would take his general guidelines and use their own initiative to select and implement several new performance measures. However, since the state devoted minimum attention to training and support, few schools took steps to implement the new measures. Some local administrators called colleagues to find out what they were doing in response to the state guidelines. When they learned that others were waiting for further direction before acting, they held up their own actions, effectively putting the entire initiative on hold.

Although leadership styles varied widely, most of the administrators we interviewed actively promoted the implementation of performance measures and standards. However, the power of individuals to influence the development and implementation of these systems in both positive and negative ways was demonstrated repeatedly.

FUTURE CONCERNS

Our ability to predict is limited, but some potential problems already seem likely. The following issues and events are likely to have a major impact on statewide systems of measures and standards in the near future. They deserve careful consideration in federal and state vocational education planning.

Skills Standards and Curriculum Standards

The Departments of Education and Labor are funding the development of industry skill standards in more than 20 occupational areas and curriculum standards in six educational fields. What will these efforts mean for statewide systems of measures and standards? Certainly, valid national standards deserve consideration by states. They might provide invaluable common criteria for occupational preparation. However, no one knows how best to accommodate such standards in systems of measures and standards, or how difficult (or expensive) such coordination might be. What supplemental work will be required to integrate industry standards and curriculum standards with state systems (e.g., connection between state occupational task lists and industry standards)? How will this work be supported?

Not only will the development of industry skill standards have an effect on statewide systems of measures and standards, but the organizations developing the industry standards need to be informed about the Perkins II measures and standards systems used in vocational education. The key question is, what effect should states' systems of measures and standards have on the structure of the industry skill standards? It is important that those developing the industry standards be aware of the accountability mechanisms states have been creating under Perkins II.

Data Quality

From 1991 to 1994, states devoted most of their energies to selecting and adopting measures and standards and developing data systems to support them. As yet, little attention has been paid to the quality of the measures and standards.[5] As soon as statewide systems become operational and programs are required to judge their performance against state standards, questions of reliability and validity will become more important. In states that adopt high stakes for performance (as in the case of Columbia), potential data quality problems will be exacerbated, because high stakes are known to corrupt the interpretation of educational data. The need for evaluations of data quality will increase once systems are fully implemented. However, states are unlikely to have the resources or expertise necessary to conduct these investigations. If these issues are not resolved, the whole enterprise may suffer, so it is important for the federal government to develop mechanisms to facilitate assessment of the quality of measures and standards.

Integration of Academic and Vocational Education

Potentially the most far-reaching reform embodied in Perkins II is the integration of academic and vocational education. This movement raises several problems for defining, measuring, and attributing outcomes and therefore threatens the validity of existing systems of measures and standards. First, states are unlikely to have included integrated outcomes in their current systems, so major changes will be required. Second, the development of measurement tools for integrated outcomes will probably lag behind the development of curriculum. Third, the conception of a vocational program will have to be changed to include academic components. Fourth, it will be difficult to attribute outcomes to specific courses and to use outcome data for program improvement. Although fully integrated programs are many years away, many states already have begun implementing some integrated academic curricula, and these states are already facing problems defining and measuring outcomes. Early attention

---

[5]This is one of the questions being addressed by the Batelle study of Perkins II. However, that study relies on data collected in 1993, before most state systems were operating on a regular basis.

to the questions raised by integrated academic and vocational education is warranted.

Consistency in Federal Vocational Education Policy

Some state vocational educators explained their less-than-enthusiastic response to Perkins II by saying, "It's going to go away." They believe new laws will supplant many of the initiatives contained in Perkins II. When implementers believe mandates are only temporary, they reduce their efforts and adopt a mind-set of minimum compliance rather than commitment. Unfortunately, the volatility of federal vocational education policy discourages rapid and effective response to federal initiatives. Long-term change is unlikely under these circumstances.

Perkins II measures and standards embody a radically different approach to accountability. It may take five years of implementation for a fair test of this initiative. However, there already is talk within the states that drastic changes in the regulations are imminent. As a result, some administrators are curbing their efforts; many are proceeding with caution. To promote effective implementation of measures and standards, the federal government must make it clear that it intends to stay the course. Further, it must give vocational educators ample time to develop, implement, and fine-tune the system before making judgments about its efficacy. A minimum of five years is required to see whether outcome-based local program improvement in the Perkins II model will work or not.

Chapter Five

RECOMMENDATIONS

This research suggests specific actions federal policymakers should take to improve the implementation of Perkins II measures and standards. Although our case studies were limited to four states, both our informal conversations with other vocational educators and previous research on the implementation of Perkins II measures and standards suggest that these concerns are widespread enough to warrant such actions. Potential responses include changes in regulations, investments in the solution of common problems, and new capacity-building initiatives at the state and local levels. These recommendations follow directly from the factors identified as being subject to federal influence in the previous chapter.

CLARIFY THE INTERRELATIONSHIPS AMONG PERKINS II MANDATES AND THE COORDINATION OF PERKINS II INITIATIVES

Perkins II requires that states emphasize systems of measures and standards, the integration of academic and vocational education, tech-prep education, and service to special populations, but it does not tell states how these activities should be interrelated, nor does it suggest how states should coordinate their efforts. As a result, states implement activities in isolation and assign them different priorities. For example, some put tech-prep education on hold while focusing on measures and standards; others assign their most talented staff to tech-prep education while delegating measures and standards to one individual.

Perkins II gives little direction to states about how to coordinate their efforts on measures and standards, tech-prep education, integration of academic and vocational education, and special populations. The omission of models for coordination decreases the potential effectiveness of the act, particularly the effectiveness of the systems of measures and standards. States need guidance regarding how to make their systems of measures and standards support their efforts to integrate academic and vocational education, create tech-prep education programs, and promote service to special populations. For example, performance measures and standards could be seen as a mechanism for evaluating all the Perkins II priorities. At present, states do not always see how the required elements can be interrelated, e.g., how needs assessment fits into the state plan, how the state plan fits with the local application process, and how the local application process fits into the annual review cycle. Neither do they see how these are all elements of an evaluation system that applies to all the Perkins II initiatives. Instead, there is wide variation in the relative priority assigned to these four critical initiatives and little coordination. Changes in the language of the legislation could clarify these relationships.

CREATE MODELS FOR OUTCOME-BASED PROGRAM IMPROVEMENT

To date, states have emphasized the "nuts and bolts" of *creating* systems of measures and standards. Over time, they need to build on this foundation and focus on *using* these systems for program improvement. At present, most state action is still driven by the mandate to develop a structure for accountability, i.e., a system of measures and standards. The law says little about how that structure is supposed to be used to make programs better. Sites must develop program improvement plans, but nothing suggests how one translates outcome deficiencies into action plans either at the local level or at the state level if the joint planning provision comes into effect. We talked to one state administrator who had begun to tackle this question by developing a set of specific questions linked to the state's measures and standards for use at a site to organize its search for improvement. However, such thought about the use of measures and standards was rare.

One way to encourage states to build toward program improvement is to require them to develop models for using outcome-based information for program reform. Certainly, it is time for states to think seriously about this phase of accountability. Yet, some states might find any additional requirements distasteful, and many would argue that additional paperwork is counterproductive. The alternative we prefer would be to commission another agency to collect examples of effective practices and disseminate them widely for states and local programs to use.

PROVIDE FOCUSED TECHNICAL ASSISTANCE REGARDING CHOICES AND RESOURCES

Perkins II gives states far greater programmatic discretion while limiting the resources they can devote to administration. This places greater demands on state administrators, but limits their capacity to act. Under these circumstances, federal actions that helped states respond to their choices and make better use of resources might significantly improve implementation of the act.

The "flexible mandates" contained in Perkins II placed demands on states and local agencies but offered no guidance in how to meet those demands. States were required to create systems of measures and standards with certain properties but were allowed considerable discretion in the design of these systems, including the choice of outcomes, the selection of measurement tools, and the setting of standards. Many lacked the expertise to make these decisions wisely. Furthermore, some states delegated many of these choices to local agencies.[1] This cascade of delegated decisionmaking placed new and unfamiliar demands on state and local staff. Few had any previous experience implementing outcome-based accountability systems in vocational education.

As a result, states looked to the U.S. Department of Education for assistance in clarifying the meaning of the regulations and providing expertise in solving problems of measurement, assessment development, and standard setting. Unfortunately, little help was offered.

---

[1] This led to considerable variation of measures and standards between states as well as large within-state variation in selected states.

The federal agency focused its resources on compliance monitoring (for all the provisions of Perkins II) rather than on providing guidance about measurement problems or acting energetically to increase a state's capacity to respond through training. Other agencies stepped in to try to address the most pressing problems (e.g., NCRVE workshops on selecting measures and setting standards). This support was helpful, but it did not satisfy the demand. Furthermore, the demand for technical assistance still exists, as many states lag behind the four we visited in implementing their systems, and some of the more difficult measurement issues remain unresolved.

A further demand for technical assistance arose within those states that delegated the choice of measures to the local level. Those with ultimate responsibility for deciding on measurement tools and procedures lacked the expertise to make these decisions and looked to the state as well as to their colleagues in other districts for assistance. The states' record in responding is mixed. Piedmont provided adequate technical assistance by training district vocational education administrators, who then trained program instructors. Erie did not.

Furthermore, we predict that a new set of technical assistance needs is on the horizon in the area of program improvement. Statewide systems will be operational on a large scale in the 1994–95 school year, and local programs will begin to compare their performance to state standards. Few at the local level have any experience using outcome data for creative program planning, so programs that do not make the grade will look to their states for guidance with program improvement. States, in turn, will turn to the federal government for assistance, for they too lack expertise in using performance measures as program-improvement tools.

The federal government should act now to address these needs by creating a mechanism for providing relevant technical assistance to states. In the long run, the goal should be to build capacity at the state level for using the standards framework as a program improvement tool. One approach might be to press for greater integration of vocational education measures and standards with existing state program review procedures. Because many states have the same questions, we believe the most efficient way to provide these services is centralized, but we would not preclude other options. Whatever the form, resources should be devoted to solving measures-and-standards problems and increasing the capacity of states to make their systems work. One state coordinator described his experience with statewide measures and standards as "trying to build a 747 in flight." Trying to do this without appropriate technical assistance and support is a prescription for failure, and much more could be done to promote success.

Resource constraints exacerbate the problem. Perkins II places greater demands on state agencies than its predecessor, but restricts the use of funds for state-level services. This comes at a time when many state administrative budgets are also being reduced. State administrators believe they lack the resources necessary to respond to Perkins II mandates effectively. These limitations are particularly severe at the postsecondary level, where some states allocate very small proportions of their Perkins II funds. Some efficiencies are possible through better coordination of efforts on measures and standards, tech-prep, integration, and special populations, and federal efforts to solve difficult measurement problems will also lessen the demands on state agencies. Furthermore, states could be encouraged to increase local participation in the technical assistance process over time, substituting regional networks and collegial assistance for some of the centralized expertise required initially.

Other resource problems might be addressed by increasing administrative allocations for certain activities. We are not advocating a return to the previous model, which many felt diverted too many dollars from students to central bureaucracies. As we see it, the need for supplemental resources and for technical assistance is not constant and can be fulfilled in many ways. Therefore, the response can be flexible. State departments of education need additional resources during times of initial development. We suggest increasing the funds available for state administration during the start-up phase, so states can meet initial demands and develop some of the expertise they will need to operate reformed vocational education systems.

ADDRESS COMMON MEASUREMENT PROBLEMS

One reason the implementation of Perkins II has been so challenging to states is that the vision embodied in the guidelines exceeds the capacity of existing measurement tools. In particular, the technology to measure learning and occupational performance in reliable, valid, and efficient ways is not widely available. For example, although much work is being done to develop performance measures of occupational skills, this is an emerging assessment area with few operational systems. The situation is worse in some areas, e.g., measuring gains in advanced academic skills appropriate for the postsecondary level, where none of the four states found existing measurement tools or had the expertise to develop their own direct measures.

Most states are not equipped to develop tools for measuring learning and occupational outcomes, and it is unfair to drop this difficult task in the lap of state vocational educators. The federal government needs to take responsibility for addressing these problems, since they are largely the result of the provisions of Perkins II.

At the same time, the federal government is supporting a variety of new assessment initiatives whose relationships to Perkins II measures and standards are unclear. These range from the development of more than 20 sets of industry skill standards to the establishment of national goals and curriculum standards for academic education. There should be some connection between the assessment demands of Perkins II and the assessment development efforts being funded separately. At a minimum, states need guidance about how the skill standards should relate to their statewide systems. Other assessment development projects to meet the specific needs of Perkins II should also be considered.

CONCLUSIONS

The 1990 amendments to the Carl D. Perkins Vocational and Applied Technology Education Act entailed major changes in federal vocational education priorities and practices. Among the most visible innovations in Perkins II is the creation of statewide systems of measures and standards of performance. The purpose of these systems is to create an objective, outcome-based framework for program evaluation that can be used as the cornerstone of local program improvement efforts. We found that states had made much progress creating the structure of measures and standards but had devoted much less attention to creating a process for using standards as program-improvement tools. We also identified a number of factors that affected state actions on measures and standards, many of which reduced the likelihood that state systems would function as envisioned in the law.

Some of these factors are subject to federal intervention, and we identified steps the federal government could take to ameliorate the situation. Incorporating these changes into the reauthorization of federal vocational education will increase the efficacy of statewide systems of measures and standards. Legislators also should anticipate difficulties and conflicts that may be created by pending reforms of education, training, and workforce preparedness programs, and they should work to coordinate the accountability requirements of all these initiatives.

STATE INTERVIEW GUIDE

RAND/MPR INTERVIEW GUIDE

Secondary/Post-Secondary Differences

Clarify the appropriate "level(s)" for the interview. Is the respondent knowledgeable about secondary vocational education, post-secondary, or both? Is s/he willing to discuss secondary issues, post-secondary or both? [Adjust questions accordingly.]

Nature of statewide measures and standards

I mailed MPR's summary description of [state's] standards and measures and asked you to update it to reflect any errors or changes. [Show document] Are any revisions necessary?

> *Are these measures or standards likely to change this year? If so, how?*

> *Are there plans to review or revise the measures / the standards in the future? If so, what will be done?*

States can use their measures and standards for many purposes, for example, evaluating instructor effectiveness; which purposes are most important in [state] at the secondary / post-secondary level?

> (Other purposes: monitoring statewide performance, holding programs accountable for outcomes, allocating resources, providing individual student information)

> *Can you rank the purposes in order of importance? How do you know?*

Importance of measures and standards vis-à-vis other vocational education initiatives

How important are measures and standards relative to other vocational education efforts?

— relative to other Perkins requirements, such as Tech Prep, integration of academic and vocational education, special populations, etc.?

— relative to other state-initiated vocational efforts?

— important in terms of actions (e.g., staff activities, resource commitments)

What kinds of activities have occurred? Can you give examples?

— important in terms of long-range impact (e.g., broader reform agenda)

Which changes will be the most lasting? Why do you think this is so?

> Note: Clarify secondary / post-secondary differences
>
> Clarify importance in terms of the interests of special populations

Would [state] have taken these actions if there had not been a federal requirement?

> *What evidence is there that [state] was moving in this direction on its own?*

Are measures and standards supportive of or antagonistic to other vocational education reform efforts?

> *Which other vocational initiatives? How are they complementary or how do they conflict?*

Integration of vocational education accountability with other educational reforms

Looking at educational reform more broadly, what are [state's] current reform efforts in general and academic education?

How do these initiatives relate to accountability in vocational education?

> For example,
>
> *Is accountability an important issue in general and academic education? What is being done to promote accountability? How have vocational education measures and standards affected this process? Why or why not?*

Is reform of assessment an important item in general and academic education? What assessment reforms are occurring? How do they relate to vocational education measures? Why or why not?

Is [state] trying to develop or improve its student data system for general and academic education? What efforts are under way? How do these relate to vocational education data collection? Why or why not? Can you identify special populations in your current data system?

Are there new programs to provide services to handicapped students, disadvantaged students or students with limited English proficiency? What is the nature of these programs? How do they relate to the requirements for service to special populations in vocational education? Why or why not?

(Possibilities: general and vocational reforms are contradictory, are not related at all, are using similar approaches but remain separate, are integrated into a single system)

Do you think vocational education accountability will play a greater or lesser role in general education reform in the future? Why?

Implementation of measures and standards

What steps have been taken to implement performance measures and standards in [state] from the time they were adopted until the present?

What have state agencies done in the areas of:

— Dissemination of information about the measures and standards?

— Staff Development and Technical Assistance?

— Data Collection?

— Reporting?

— Monitoring state and local actions?

Which agencies/personnel have been involved?

What actions have they taken?

How do these activities differ from the activities they were doing in the past?

What level of resources is being devoted to the implementation of standards and measures? (e.g., How many staff are involved?)

What have local programs done in these same areas? How does this differ from what they did in the past?

What are the major problems that have been encountered in implementing measures and standards?

How have attitudes toward measures and standards changed as the system has been developed and implemented? Improved? Grown more hostile?

Technical issues regarding measures and standards

What is the state doing to assess the reliability and fairness of the measures?

> *Do you have any specific information about the quality of the measures?*

How important is comparability of data between programs?

> *Will your system provide comparable data at the program level? How do you know?*

What is the state doing to assess the validity of the standards?

> *How were standards set?*

> *Do you plan to review or revise the standards in the future?*

Do you permit local modifications to standards? Why or why not? If so, how well are they working?

What is being done to encourage service to special populations?

> *Are you using incentives or adjustments? Why or why not?*

Use of measures and standards

How are measures and standards supposed to be used at the state level (e.g., for monitoring, accountability, funding)?

> *How will they be reported, and to whom?*

> *What use will be made of the information?*

How are measures and standards supposed to be used at the local level (e.g., for student counseling, program improvement)?

> *How will data be reported, and to whom?*

> *What use will be made of the information?*

> *What is the state doing to affect the local use of this information?*

Are people concerned about the possible abuse of the measures and standards (e.g., creating incentives for programs to admit only the most qualified students)?

> *What problems do you foresee? Why or why not?*

Assistance and Support for Measures and Standards

What kinds of technical support do state offices need to implement measures and standards (e.g., specialized training)?

> *Have you tried to obtain outside support? From whom?*

What kinds of technical assistance is needed at the local level?

> *What is the state doing to provide it?*

What support will be provided specifically to encourage the use of measures and standards for local program improvement?

> *What is the state's role in local program improvement?*

Effects of measures and standards

What effects have the measures and standards had so far (e.g., shifting responsibility from the state to the local level)?

— on state agencies?

— on local programs?

— on the relationship between state agencies and local programs?

What are the advantages and disadvantages of standards from the point of view of:

— your agency?

— other state agencies?

— local programs?

— business and industry?

LOCAL INTERVIEW GUIDE

RAND/MPR Interview Guide

Visits to Local Districts

Notes

Respondents have been classified into categories, and sections of the interview are assigned to specific types of respondents:

- Superintendent—includes state, district and college chief administrators, e.g., chief state school officer, superintendent, chancellor, president.

- Principal—includes local school chief administrators, e.g., principal, assistant principal.

- Vocational Director—includes district or college vocational administrator, e.g., director of vocational education, vocational coordinator.

- Teacher—includes college instructors and secondary teachers.

- Other—includes administrators responsible for placement, special education, evaluation, data systems, etc.

The general term "institution" is used in the interview guide. Substitute "state," "district," "college" or "school" as appropriate to the particular interview.

RAND/MPR Interview Guide

Visits to Local Districts

PERFORMANCE MEASURES AND STANDARDS [SUPERINTENDENT, PRINCIPAL]

Adjust questions for standards and measures as implemented in each state, e.g., centralized vs. decentralized.

Are you familiar with your state's performance measures and standards? (Ask by measure category) • Basic and advanced academic skills • Occupational competency • Job or work skill attainment • Retention • Placement • Other [decentralized] Which specific measures and standards has your institution adopted?	• When was the first time you were introduced to these measures and standards? • Were you involved in their development? • Has your institution added measures and standards to the state's set? • How did you decide what to adopt? • Who participated in the process?

THE NATURE AND USE OF STATEWIDE MEASURES AND STANDARDS [SUPERINTENDENT, PRINCIPAL]

For what purposes will measures and standards be used in your institution (*local level*)? (e.g., for student counseling, program improvement)	• How will data be reported, and to whom? • How will the information be used? • Will the information be used to compare programs?
How will the data you report be used at the state level? (e.g., for monitoring, accountability, funding)	• How will the data be reported, and to whom? • How will the information be used? • Will the information be used to compare programs or institutions? • How has the state communicated its intentions to you?
Are people in this institution concerned about the possible abuse of measures and standards? (e.g., creating incentives for programs to admit only the most qualified students)	• Who has expressed concern? Why? • What problems do you foresee? • Why or why not?

IMPORTANCE OF MEASURES AND STANDARDS VIS-A-VIS OTHER VOCATIONAL EDUCATION INITIATIVES [VOCATIONAL DIRECTOR]

Which vocational education reforms or initiatives have received the most emphasis in your institution in the past two years?	
How important are measures and standards in your institution relative to — other Perkins requirements, such as Tech Prep, integration of academic and vocational education, special populations, etc.? — other state initiated vocational efforts? — district initiated vocational efforts? — school site initiated vocational efforts?	• What activities have occurred that justify your judgment? • Can you give specific examples? • Which of these reforms will be more lasting? • Why do you think this is so?
How do measures and standards relate to the local program application process? How do they fit in to the annual program evaluation process? How do the federal requirements differ from preexisting state policies or procedures?	• What do you do differently now than you did prior to measures and standards? • How have reporting requirements changed under Perkins I and Perkins II?
Are measures and standards supportive of or antagonistic to other vocational education reform efforts?	• Which other vocational reforms? • How are they complementary or how do they conflict?

INTEGRATION OF VOCATIONAL EDUCATION ACCOUNTABILITY WITH OTHER EDUCATIONAL REFORMS [SUPERINTENDENT, PRINCIPAL]

In education more broadly, which recent reform activities have received the most attention in your institution?	• How do these initiatives relate to accountability in vocational education?
Is accountability an important aspect of general education reform?	• What is being done to promote accountability? • How have vocational education measures and standards affected or been affected by this process? • Why or why not?
Would the institution have taken actions to create or improve an accountability system without the federal requirement?	• What evidence is there that the institution was moving in this direction on its own? • What changes in assessment would have occurred? • What changes in data collection and use would have occurred?
Is reform of assessment an important item in general education? In vocational education?	• What assessment reforms are occurring? • How do they relate to vocational education measures? • Why or why not?
Is the institution trying to develop or improve its student data system for general education?	• What efforts are under way? • How do these efforts relate to vocational education data collection? Why or why not? • How are special populations identified? • How are tech prep students identified? • How do you define a "vocational student?"
Are there new programs to provide services to handicapped students, disadvantaged students or students with limited English proficiency?	• What is the nature of these programs? • How do they relate to the requirements for service to special populations in vocational education? • Why or why not?

| Do you think vocational education accountability will play a greater or lesser role in general education reform in the future? | • Why? |

IMPLEMENTATION OF MEASURES AND STANDARDS
[SUPERINTENDENT, VOCATIONAL DIRECTOR, PRINCIPAL]

Do the measures and standards apply to individual programs or to vocational education as a whole? Which local programs will be evaluated based on measures and standards?	• Did you choose to concentrate Perkins funds on a limited number of sites or on a limited number of vocational programs? • Does the accountability system only apply to the projects, services, and activities assisted by Perkins funds? Or will measures and standards be applied more broadly to other programs? • Who is going to be required to report data?
What steps have been taken to implement performance measures and standards from the time they were adopted until the present?	• Which agencies or personnel have been involved? • What actions were taken? • Has your district added measures and standards to those adopted by the state?
Who will be responsible for implementing the performance measures and standards?	• What responsibilities does this include? • Who else will be involved in the process? • What level of resources is being devoted to implementation?
How much discretion do you have in how you implement the measures and standards?	• What changes have you made, or could you make? • What supplemental requirement have you imposed?
What are the major problems that have been encountered in implementing measures and standards?	• What local conditions have been a barrier to implementation? • What has changed in the area of assessment and data collection? • How reasonable is the timeline required by the state?

What is being done to encourage service to special populations?	• Does the system include incentives or adjustments to encourage service? • How do your programs monitor and insure access, retention, and completion of special populations?
How are performance measures and standards linked with the annual program evaluation? How are performance measures and standards involved in the program application process? Do performance measures and standards play a role in other Perkins requirements?	• What is the connection between performance measures and standards and the annual evaluation? • What is the connection between performance measures and standards and the yearly application process for Perkins funds? • What other new Perkins data requirements have come from the state? • What new special population data requirements are there? • What are you doing to identify barriers to access or success and to evaluate the progress of special populations? • What are you doing to monitor teaching "all aspects of the industry?"
Under what circumstances will you be required to write a local improvement plan ?	• What directions has the state given you for developing a local improvement plan? • Who is responsible for determining improvement? • What is meant in this state by "substantial progress" toward achieving standards? • Who decided on the definition of this term?

Effects of Measures and Standards [Superintendent, Principal, Vocational Director]

What changes have occurred in program evaluation procedures as a result of measures and standards? —in staff evaluation procedures? —in student evaluation procedures?	How are programs/staff/students evaluated? How has this process changed in the past two years? What caused these changes? (Perkins or other factors) How will it change this year or next? [collect examples of relevant documents]
What changes have occurred in data collection or data reporting? What changes are anticipated in the future?	Which data do teachers and administrators use to judge the quality of programs? Have there been changes in the available data during the past two years? If so, which data are no longer used, which are newly available? Will there be changes this year or next? [collect examples of relevant reports]
What changes have occurred in staff responsibilities as a result of measures and standards? What changes are anticipated in the future?	How many staff are involved with measures and standards? What do they do? What additional roles or responsibilities will evolve in the future?
Have measures and standards created any additional burdens for administrators or staff? Any other problems?	What other demands do measures and standards make? What other problems have occurred?
Do you have a Technical Advisory Group or something similar? How have measures and standards affected the role of the Technical Advisory Group?	• How often does it meet? • Who participates? • Have there been any changes in the nature or function of the group? Why?

How have attitudes toward measures and standards changed as the system has been implemented?	• What were your first reactions? Other people's reactions? • How have those changed? • Can you give examples?
Have you had to write any program improvement plans?	• What criteria did you use to identify sites requiring program improvement plans? • What actions did the plans include? [collect examples of relevant documents]
What effects have the measures and standards had so far on (e.g., shifting responsibility from the state to the local level): — state agencies? — local programs? — the relationship between state agencies and local programs?	
What are the advantages and disadvantages of measures and standards from the point of view of: — district? — local programs? — business and industry?	
What do you anticipate the effects will be on program planning and instruction?	• What kinds of changes might you make based on the data? • What kind of training or support would you need to use the data effectively? [collect examples of relevant documents]
What effects will performance measures and standards have on special populations?	• What steps have been taken to monitor access, progress, or success of special populations in quality vocational programs? • Are you applying the same standards to all programs, or separate standards for special populations? • Have the special populations served under Perkins changed over the past two years?

TECHNICAL ASSISTANCE AND SUPPORT FOR MEASURES AND STANDARDS [VOCATIONAL DIRECTOR]

What technical assistance has been provided by the state? by the district?	
What kinds of technical support do districts/schools/institutions need to implement measures and standards? (e.g., specialized training)	• Have you tried to obtain outside support? • From whom? • What is the state doing to provide it? • How is the state receiving the information on what technical assistance/support the local level needs?
What are the most effective vehicles for technical assistance at the local level? (e.g., guidebooks, workshops, conferences, electronic mail, etc.)	• Has the state held workshops? the district? • Have you attended AVA or other national conferences? • Do you receive information from NCRVE?
What support will be provided specifically to encourage the use of measures and standards for local program improvement?	• What is the state's role in local program improvement? the district's role? the school's role? the teacher's role?

"GRASS-ROOTS" ISSUES [TEACHER]

• How do you evaluate your program? • Do you have a Technical Advisory Group or something similar?	• What kinds of data are collected? • How are the data used to judge the quality of programs and instructional strategies? • Is this a burden on you or your program? • What are you doing this year that is different than two years ago? • Does it play a role in program evaluation? • If so, how often does it meet and who participates? • How long has the group been around? • Have there been any changes in the nature or function of the group? Why?
Are you familiar with your state's performance measures and standards? (Ask by measure category) • Basic and advanced academic skills • Occupational competency • Job or work skill attainment • Retention • Placement • Other	• When was the first time you were introduced to these measures and standards? • Were you involved in their development?
How have performance measures and standards affected you or your program? What do you anticipate the effects will be on program planning and instruction in the future?	• Have they changed the way you evaluate the program? If so, how? • Have they changed the data you collect, report or use? If so, how? • Have they changed staff responsibilities? If so, in what ways? • Have they created additional burdens or other problems? If so, please describe.
How useful will performance measures and standards be for measuring the effectiveness of your program?	• Will measures and standards help you improve your program? In what way? • Will measures and standards be used to compare your program to other programs? If yes, how do you feel about that?

What assistance do you think you need in order to make the data useful?	• What assistance have you received From whom? • Has the state held workshops? the district? • What kind of technical assistance is most helpful to you? (e.g., guidebooks, workshops, conferences, electronic mail, etc.) • Have you attended AVA or other national conferences? • Do you receive information from NCRVE?
What does your program do to encourage service to special populations?	• How do you monitor and ensure access, retention, and completion of special populations? • Have the types of special populations you serve changed over the past two years?

Berman, P., and M. W. McLaughlin, *Federal Programs Supporting Educational Change:* Vol. VIII, *Implementing and Sustaining Innovations*, Santa Monica, Calif.: RAND, R-1589/9-HEW, 1978.

Hoachlander, E. G., K. Levesque, and M. L. Rahn, *Accountability for Vocational Education: A Practitioner's Guide*, Berkeley, Calif.: National Center for Research in Vocational Education, MDS-407, 1992.

Rahn, M. L., and M. Alt, "Performance Standards and Measures," Chapter 2 in *National Assessment of Vocational Education Final Report to Congress*, Vol. III, *Program Improvement: Education Reform*, Washington D.C.: U.S. Department of Education, Office of Educational Research and Improvement, Office of Research, July 1994.

Rahn, M. L., E. G. Hoachlander, and K. Levesque, *State Systems for Accountability in Vocational Education.* Berkeley, Calif.: National Center for Research in Vocational Education, MDS-491, 1992.

Stecher, B. M., and L. M. Hanser, *Beyond Vocational Education Standards and Measures: Strengthening Local Accountability Systems for Program Improvement*, Berkeley, Calif.: National Center for Research in Vocational Education, MDS-292, 1993. (Also available from RAND as R-4282-NCRVE/UCB, 1993.)

U.S. Congress, Carl D. Perkins Vocational and Applied Technology Education Act Amendment of 1990, P.L. 101-392, September 25, 1990.

U.S. Congress, *Student Right-to-Know and Campus Security Act,* P.L. 101-542, November 8, 1990.